MEDITATION FOR BEGINNERS

A BEGINNER'S GUIDE TO THE HISTORY, IMPORTANCE, AND HOW-TO OF MEDITATION

Copyright © 2014 by Justin Albert

Why You Should Read This Book

What is the only thing obstructing you from achieving all of your dreams, feeling interior happiness, and living a mindful, productive life?

What is currently the center of your universe, hindering your appropriate view of yourself, creating fears and anxieties that are completely eliminating all goodness you deserve to have?

Your mind, of course.

You need to find a method to parse through the intricacies of your mind, to better understand yourself on a deeper, intimate level.

Meditation gives you alarming insight about one of the most mysterious elements of yourself: your inner thoughts. It allows you to dive into your mind, walk through the strange, hidden rooms of yourself, and discover what you've been hiding from yourself and from the rest of the world. You can discover why you're afraid of things, why you self-sabotage, and why your continuous stressors are making you crazy.

Meditation is one of the oldest formations of religion. It actually pre-dates history. It's been thought, even, that some aspects of meditation were formulated by people in caves gazing at their fires, thinking about the depth of their lives. (If you've ever gazed into a fire and NOT thought about the greatness of the universe, you need to work to broaden your mind a little, anyway.)

In this rushing mentality of the twenty-first century, however, it isn't very often that we pause and think about our lives, about our minds, or even about our bodies (unless we're looking to alter our weight, gain muscle, or do anything to "boost" our rank in society, of course).

We are constantly moving around, constantly working, and, in return, we are actually killing ourselves. We are creating our own cancers, our own heart diseases, our own depressions, and our own anxieties.

We need to stop.

Just two to five minutes of meditation per day has been scientifically proven to boost brain development. It has been proven to alter your state of mind, to keep you better organized, to fuel interior happiness, and to create a better mentality about your surrounding world. As a result of meditation, you can hold more empathy for both yourself and others. You can begin to treat yourself and those you love with better care, with more earnestness, and with enhanced, enriched feeling.

Furthermore, you can better understand your goals in life. You can work through the battered and bruised parts of your mind to inhabit internal strength, to be not so quick to anger, and to become a stronger, better version of yourself.

Turn to meditation, the ancient art of "knowing one's self" to truly get to the heart of your life. Don't go through your day-to-day blind to the mysteries of your mind. Know yourself. Find strength in yourself. And then: proceed out into the world rooted to that comprehension.

TABLE OF CONTENTS

Why You Should Read This Book

Table of Contents

Chapter 1. The Intricacies and Long History of Meditation

Chapter 2. Ancient Rituals and Formations of Meditation

Chapter 3. Meditation and the Brain: The Dramatic Research

Chapter 4. Learning to Meditate: For Beginners

Chapter 5. Making Meditation a Habit

Chapter 6. Overarching Benefits and Long-Standing Reasons Why You Should Meditate for Life

About The Author

Other Books By : Justin Albert

Chapter 1. The Intricacies and Long History of Meditation

Meditation allows you to alter your state of mind, to fuel yourself with the interior power to flip your current perception of the world. People all over, from country to country turn to meditation to calm themselves, to relieve their anxieties, to soften their anger, and to face the "human condition" without alarming fear. Essentially, meditation allows you to live your life better, without all the bumps along the way.

As you practice meditation, its power comes over you to rejuvenate you and create interior, emotional positivity and an ability to concentrate. In a sense, through meditation, you begin to learn yourself better simply by sitting and engaging—or watching—your mind, as if from a distance. You begin to understand the intricacies of what's going on behind your own eyes, the reasons you do everything you do, and how you can alter everything you do and the reasons you do them through a different, more engaged state of mind. How interesting, isn't it, to note that you perhaps don't know yourself so well?

With practice and patience, you can create a meditative peace about you that can work to help you make positive, life-affirming choices and transform your life for the better.

Note that simply reading about meditation will not yield this mindfulness and sense of peace. You must practice what you learn in order to "dig" into your unconscious mind and draw these powerful outcomes.

History of Meditation

People began practicing meditation before they began recording dates and events. Therefore, essentially, the beginning of meditation is "prehistoric." It lurks in the dates before history. Note that this initial meditation was very much religious-based in that people worked to create repetitive chants, which today are referred to as "mantras." Since this quite ancient beginning date, meditation has evolved into something we utilize all the time, daily, in order to initiate better survival strategies in our lives.

Initial 1500 B.C.E. records of meditation discuss something called Dhyana, a type of meditation that is based in Hindu tradition. Note that this was around the time that yoga was first initially recorded, as the Hindu tradition natural linked the two together. After around one thousand years, these initial traditions paved the way for Taoist and Buddhist meditation, in China. Also during this time, something called the Yoga Sutras of Patajali was completed, which formulated eight limbs of yoga—which paves the way toward more modern utilizations of yoga. Furthermore, the Bhagavad Gita was created during this time, which is a sort of scripture based in the art of meditation, yoga, and spirituality.

A Note on the Bhagavad Gita

In English, the Bhagavad Gita literally means The Song of the Bhagavan. It is a 700-verse song and Hindu-based scripture found in a greater book, a Hindu epic called the Mahbharata. The sixth chapter of the Bhagavad Gita brings essential translation to the purpose of meditation.

The Bhagavad Gita states the phrase: "Dhyanenatmani pasyanati kecidatmanamaatmana, which essentially means that as a yogi, you are meant to perceive yourself inside of yourself utilizing meditation. Through this, the meditation practitioner is meant to claim all control over his body and his mind and remove his interior desires.

Meditation's Growth Around the World

Buddhist meditation was first recorded in about 100 B.C. After this date, the Silk Road transmission of Buddhism, which allows Buddhism to spread throughout Asia, brought meditation to many other countries, like India and Nepal. Furthermore, there's sufficient evidence noting that the Torah, the Jewish religious text, brought meditative practices from the Silk Road into its scripture. There is a central idea in Judaism that is relevant to the historical context of meditation. Even their current prayer has glimmers of meditative practices and repetitions.

During the eighth century, Japanese Buddhism bloomed. This was during the time that a Japanese monk named Dosho learned about Zen during his sojourn to China in the 600's. When he returned back to Japan, he opened an initial meditation practice hall in Nara. These first meditation practices in Japan were open to change, and they did so in the next 600 years.

The Islamic religion further looks to meditation to hold remembrance of God, and history shows that this began in the 12th century. The meditation practices worked to match this meditation with something called fikr, which is a formation of "thinking." The match of both meditation and fikr was said to create essential knowledge and holiness.

Furthermore, even some Eastern versions of Christianity utilize meditation and repetition. This was especially found in Greece, during something called hesychasm, which occurs on Mount Athos in Greece to this day. This brings continuous repetition of the Christian Jesus prayer.

Note that Western Christian meditation refutes all former religious, meditation practices in that it does not hold repetition to commute a sort of higher understanding.

Modern-Day Meditation

Modern-day meditation began in the 18th century, when Buddhist culture was a rampant cultural conversation in both Western Europe and the United States. Famous French writer asked his readers to tolerate Buddhists, and a philosopher named Schopenhauer discussed the intricacies of the practice. Something called The Tibetan Book of the Dead was initially published in English in the 1920's, bringing much of this culture into the Western comprehension for the first time.

The Hindu revivalism began in about 1890. This had a lot to do with the fact that Britain was colonizing India and soaking up some of the culture. Note that after this time, there was a great deal of meditation-based social reform, with the work of Mahatma Gandhi, Bab Amte, and Vinoba Bhave.

Furthermore, in 1893, a man named Vivekananda, who was an Indian sami, came to the World Parliament of Religions, based in Chicago. He brought an incredible message about uniting all world religions, and he altered the state of mind of everyone present. Through his message, he paved a wide road for more and more Hindu, meditative teachers to go the United States.

Meditation and World War II

Post World War II, many soldiers returned back to the United States after spending time in the Pacific countries. Note that many of these men had actually thrived with the culture of those unique countries. The philosophies of the Japanese warrior, the samurai, found themselves woven into the hearts and minds of many servicemen, allowing them to breathe meditation practices and hold better Buddhist understanding of both life and death.

Some of these servicemen didn't even come back. Instead, they stayed on in Japan and joined monasteries in order to better understand Zen. Through Zen, they were able to deal with the enormous horrors they had endured during the Second World War. Going back to the United States would not have offered them the same understanding. Note that the past sixty to seventy years, after the horrors of World War II, has opened up the strange world of mental disorders. Before, they were nothing—never talked about. But now, with the assurance of many servicemen suicide, the United States and the western world must turn to mental disease and acknowledge it. Meditation is one of the best formations of treatment.

Post-World War II and Today

The meditation traditions based in Tibet, China, India, and Japan fueled their way into modern writers of the twentieth century. Find them rampant in writings by Allan Ginsberg and Jack Kerouac, for example. *The Dharma Bums*, by Kerouac, became essential literature for the "beat generation." During these decades, the 50's and the 60's, medical practitioners and psychologists began to learn about the intricate ways of the mind and the amazing alterations that could be formulated simply with meditation and strength of the unconscious.

During the 60's, two books were published called *The Art of Living* and *The Science of Begin*, both written by an unknown Indian named Maharishi Mahesh Yogi. Through these books, he discussed something truly revolutionary to the rest of the world: transcendental meditation. From this book, a transcendental universe was formed. Even the Beatles, a four-part band who initially wanted to "hold your hand" were suddenly following the ways of transcendental meditation. Because they had made everything else popular, the Beatles also made transcendental meditation popular for the masses.

Soon, the Dalai Lama was being quoted everywhere. The meditative comprehension of the east had fully stormed into the west. Meditation was suddenly as understandable as pop music (on a surface level, of course). Thankfully, meditation was for everyone.

Chapter 2. Ancient Rituals and Formations of Meditation

Meditation, as old as time itself, has evolved and altered over the years to formulate many different "species," many different paths to inner peace. Look to the following for examples of some of the most essential meditation formations.

Mindfulness Meditation

Mindfulness meditation, often called Vipassan, is perhaps the most essential, often-utilized formation of Buddhist meditation, especially in the Western tradition. With mindfulness meditation, you learn to accept your internal thoughts. You watch them as they pass through you; you are non-judgmental of them. You do not necessarily act on them; you do not refute them, either. You look at them as something "other" than yourself.

In some cases, this can allow you to separate your physical experiences from your emotions about those experiences. Therefore, if you have a traumatic experience, or are quick to rise in anger, you can pause, understand what you're thinking and what your emotions are, and slice a line through your mind, separating your physical self from these emotions. This can be very important to formulate a stable, well-formed life.

Zazen

Zazen was once a generalized term that encompassed the sheer fact that much of Buddhist meditation was formulated when you were sitting. However, modernized Zen brings zazen meditation, which is minimal meditation that can be done for very long lengths of time. There aren't very many instructions for the zazen meditation scope, which makes it really nice for people looking to "dip their toes" into the meditation sphere. Essentially, they must sit with their back straight. That's it. During this time, they do not have to concentrate or focus on their breathing or alter their breathing in any way.

For many, zazen is utilized alongside another focus, when one concentrates completely on a paradoxical sentence (referred to as a koan) or a scripture. Note further that zazen on its own—without this other focus—is often very difficult to lead you on the path to "enlightenment" because it has a sheer lack of guidance from outside meditative personas. This is why, for beginners, many meditation experts recommend mindfulness meditation.

Kundalini

This Vedenta, or Hindu-based tradition of meditation, is based off the Hindu name for the interior life, or the interior energy inside of your body. (Note that according to Hindu practices, there is an "upward" stream of interior, bodily energy and a downward stream of interior energy.) Kundalini meditation works to make you aware of your interior, upward stream and to ride this stream upward, into a state of enlightenment or infinity.

During this kundalini meditation, then, you work to "follow" your breath in your body through the various energy centers. You feel the energy through the center of your hips, the center of your belly, the center of your chest, the center of your throat, the center of your head, to the center of the top of your head. You follow that energy to infinity to achieve inner peace.

Transcendental Meditation

Transcendental meditation, made popular in western tradition in the 1960's time of enlightenment, is also based from Hindu tradition. During transcendental meditation, you work to sit with your back straight—sort of like zazen. However, you also utilize a mantra, or a spiritual or sacred word that you continually repeat to yourself in your conscious mind.

The focus of transcendental meditation is to target your mind's thoughts far above the impermanence of the universe. Note that transcendental meditation is far more difficult than either mindfulness meditation or zazen. When you work yourself up in the transcendental meditation abilities, you are able to focus on your breath and alter your breath in order to alter your interior emotions and feelings. Therefore, your breathing can have ultimate control.

In its most advanced stages of transcendental meditation, you are actually able to leave your body (think "transcendental," or transcending into an otherness) in order to see the world and yourself with a different perspective.

Qi Gong Meditation

Qi gong meditation is a Taoist-based meditation that utilizes the circulation of your breath to wrap your energy throughout the various energy centers and bodily organs of your physical being. It does this through a specific pattern known as the microcosmic orbit.

During Qi Gong meditation, you work to focus completely on your breath and the circulation of this breath, which is known as your chi. Furthermore, you focus on three other points: a point approximately two inches beneath your belly button, the very middle of your chest, and the very middle of your forehead. (Note that these are all vast energy centers according to tradition.)

Trance-Based Meditation

Trance-based meditative practices actually do exist in the world, and not just in cartoons or crime thrillers. During trance-based meditative practices, you are mostly unaware of your surrounding environment and yourself. You don't have complete control of your bodily experience. You further do not think rationally, and you do not have memory of the experience. Sometimes, these trance-based meditations work to help you "learn" something about yourself, reveal that thing to someone else, or dig into your deeper unconscious mind. Note that generally speaking, these trance-based meditations are created utilizing music, drugs, fast and quick rabbit-like breathing. (They are not formulated, then, utilizing the swing of a yo-yo.)

When you don't have self-control via this trance-based meditation, you are automatically in a dangerous state—a danger to both yourself and others. Furthermore, when someone ELSE gives you this passivity, you are further at danger and not along the path to enhanced spiritual development.

Therefore, trance-based meditative practices are best avoided unless a doctor is orchestrating them. Trances are not to be played around with.

The Difference Between Mindfulness of Breathing and Loving-Kindness Meditations

Both mindfulness of breathing meditation and loving-kindness meditation were cultivated originally by the first, historic Buddha. The mindfulness of breathing meditation utilizes breathing as the ultimate object of your mind's concentration. As you begin to focus only on your breath, you begin to notice how strange your mind and your stream of consciousness is. You notice how helter-skelter your thoughts become, jumping from one subject to another. This constant jumping is disallowing interior peace. As you concentrate only on your breath, you allow yourself to "practice" this innate concentration that is so essential to truly create peace. Through this concentration, you create something known as "dhyana," which is the ultimate formation of meditation, according to Hinduism.

Note that this simple idea of concentrating only on your breath, even if you don't have a means to a "meditation" state yet, can be an essential way to calm yourself during an anxiety attack. Therefore, it can be a tool you take with you everywhere: from the subway to your difficult, holiday family dinners.

On the other side of mindfulness of breathing is loving-kindness meditation. Through long kindness meditation, you work to bring "bare attention" to yourself; therefore, you allow yourself to be open to anything, you allow the entire world to bring insight to you. Therefore, in a sense, loving kindness meditation is the direct opposite of FOCUSING on your stream of consciousness via mindfulness meditation. You are not focusing on any one thing. Instead, you are leaving yourself open, like an empty piece of paper for anything to write on.

Furthermore, during loving-kindness, you are meant to fuel yourself with ideas of altruistic of selfless love for those around you. You are meant to heal yourself of your past traumas and bring "sweet" thoughts of both loving and kindness to your brain.

The Extensions of Loving-Kindness Meditation

Note that according to some Buddhist practices, loving-kindness meditation is actually the first rank in a series of many meditations that yield the following love qualities: compassion, also known as karuna, friendliness, also known as metta, equanimity, also known as upekkha, and appreciative joy, also known as mudita.

According to tradition, the order goes: friendliness, which can mature into compassion. Afterwards, compassion can fuel itself into empathy, which ultimately brings appreciative joy—because you appreciate everything that others go through, no matter if it's bad or good. After appreciative joy comes equanimity, which means you feel equality of love and kindness and acceptance in all aspects of your life and the lives of others.

Understanding and Choosing Koans

As mentioned previously, a koan is utilized in meditation often in order to fuel an enhanced meditative state. But what is a koan, exactly?

A koan is a short statement, a short story, or a short parable. It can be just a few words, or it can be a few paragraphs. The koans are generally formulated from the teachings of the Buddha. When you meditate on a koan, you are meant to transcend from your daily mind, your daily thoughts in order to arrive into an enlightened place in your head. It is essential to note that these koans are not exactly "solvable." As a result, you are meant to ponder them, think through them, and never really come out on the other side of "understanding" them. The sayings are experiences rather than traditional sayings that reek of knowledge.

Note that rationally or intellectually, it can be difficult to wrap your mind around the "point" of the koan.

For example, one of the most traditional koans is the following:

"WHAT IS THE SOUND OF ONE HAND CLAPPING."

If you come at this koan from an intellectual perspective, what would you say? Probably, you would say that a single hand wouldn't make any sound at all. And, I suppose, that would be correct in the natural world.

However, people who generally practice Zen koan would state, instead, that you must experience the above question instead of "think about it." You must put yourself into a meditative state and dwell "inside" the question. When you are able to look at the question in a meditative state, rather than with a rational mind, you are closest to finding the answer to the question.

Note that koans can be found outside of the Buddhist religion. According to many people, the teachings of the Christian's Jesus Christ exhibited many koans with his parable work. For example, Jesus said:

"To you it has been given to know the mysteries of the kingdom of God, but to the rest it is given in parables, that 'Seeing they may not see, and hearing they may not understand.'"

Coming from this realistically, this saying doesn't do much for you. Seeing they may not see, and hearing they may not understand? But Christians will tell you that you must meditate on the saying, that you must pray to better understand it. You do not come to greater inner peace through realistic thinking. You do so through higher comprehension, through a feeling of higher power.

Chapter 3. Meditation and the Brain: the Dramatic Research

As mentioned previously, the concept of meditation is as old as society itself. However, with the broadening and strength of science, humanity has begun to define meditation in a different way during the past sixty years. Through research, scientists have been able to understand the unique effects of meditation on the body—the very processes that occur as a result of meditation. The research gives dramatic backing to the benefits of meditation.

The initial research began in the 1950's with many hundreds of studies. Many of these beginner studies have since been deemed flawed. However, they brought the research into the minds of future scientist and researchers, eager to find a conclusion. What is going on in there?

After many years of enhanced technology, finally we've arrived at the dramatic fMRI scans that allow us to better understand what's actually going on inside your head when you meditate and in the hours, days, and weeks after you begin the meditation processes.

The Brain on Meditation

Once you begin the meditation habit, through the aforementioned two-minute per day practices, you can begin to initiate into the overall brain-led benefits of meditation. Most notably, meditation alters the brain on a significant level, allowing you to ward off disease, anxiety, and depression.

Scientists have utilized fMRI scans in order to understand what's actually going on inside your noggin when you meditate. The general, overarching difference in meditating brain versus a non-meditating brain lies in the fact that themeditating brain halts so much activity and processes. The beta waves begin to decrease, as well, which notes that you're processing less and less information. This occurs after every meditation session, even your very first one! (Giving you no excuse not to start today.)

Note what occurs in the specific parts of your brain below:

1. *YOUR FRONTAL LOBE ON MEDITATION.*

The frontal lobe is the most active, most constantly-revving part of your brain. It's the part of your brain in which you have your self-conscious awareness, your reasoning, your ability to plan, and all of your emotions—both negative and positive.

And when you meditate, your frontal lobe—this constantly rushing part of your brain—actually shuts off. It just stops working. It's gone. You don't have to deal with those things for a while. Isn't that nice?

2. *YOUR THALAMUS ON MEDITATION.*

The thalamus is the part of your brain that brings sensory data into the brain from the rest of your body. Therefore, everything you see, hear, touch, etc. has to enter your brain through the thalamus, and the thalamus can actually pick and choose what your brain gets to decipher.

When you meditate, the incoming sensory information is slowed incredibly. The thalamus gets a much-needed break.

You no longer have to decipher everything that's happening around you. You can just be.

3. Your Parietal Love on Meditation.

Your parietal lobe is the part of the brain that takes what your thalamus gives your brain and processes it in order to tell you how and where you exist in your environment and in your time. Therefore, it is perhaps one of the most important parts of your brain. It is the brain that tells you who and where you are.

When you meditate, however, your parietal lobe activity decreases incredibly. You no longer have to think about your age—however alarmingly high or low it might be when compared to others. You no longer have to think about where you live—no matter if that place is not such a wonderful, beneficial place. You can just exist—whoever "you" are.

4. Your Reticular Formation on Meditation.

Your reticular formation brings visual stimuli into the brain and allows the brain to be continually alert, like a soldier.

However, when you meditate, the signal for your brain to remain alert falls away. You are no longer open to as many stimuli, which is important. You have to give your brain a rest and allow it to cool down.

Benefits as a Result of these Reduced Brain Processes

Now that you understand how meditation affects your brain and works to relieve your many brain organs, you can better understand how it brings ready relief to the rest of you—through these released brain processes.

1. DECREASED LEVELS OF ANXIETY.

When you meditate every day, habitually, you have decreased levels of anxiety. This is because when you meditate often, you're actually disconnecting or altering the interior neural pathways in your head. While this sounds like you're damaging your brain, you're actually not. You're giving it room to breathe.

Essentially, when you don't meditate, you have a section of your brain known as the medial prefrontal cortex that many call the "Me Center." This essential part of your brain formulates and processes the information from the surrounding world that relates to both your experiences and to you, as a person. Generally speaking, the neural pathways you currently have from your sensations and your fear brain centers to these Me centers are very, very strong. Therefore, when you are scared or upset, you have a serious reaction in your Me center. This makes you feel like you're under attack when something just might have upset you or scared you a little bit, in real life. (It just puts a different reality on your actual surroundings. Interesting, no?)

However, when you meditate often, you work to loosen this connection between the fear centers to the Me centers. Therefore, when you are scared in the future, you won't completely freak out as a result. Your Me center won't activate in the same way. Essentially, you're just turning the electricity down to save energy.

When you weaken this neural connection, you work to strengthen the connection between these fear centers and your Assessment center, or the part of your brain that allows you to reason well. Therefore, when you're scared or upset, you can link those feelings with reason and understand that you should or shouldn't be that scared. (This is something you were unable to do with your previous "strength" wires between fear and ME.)

A good example for how this works goes like this:

You feel a pain in your side. In the days of pre-meditation, you'll feel the pain and immediately link it to "you." You'll start thinking: "Oh, maybe I have cancer. Maybe I have a growth. Maybe something bad is going to happen to me."

When you meditate often, however, you eliminate those signals. Instead, you learn to experience the pain as something outside of "you." You watch your pain and you don't make up a story about the pain. It's just something that's happening to your body, and you don't have to get bogged down about the fear of it. You have greater reason about the pain.

2. GREATER ABILITY TO FOCUS.

When you learn to meditate often, you orchestrate a higher level of concentration and focus. Note that, as your mother said, practice does make perfect. Therefore, as you learn to concentrate and focus on your breathing, on your body, watching your thoughts flow through your head, you'll learn to concentrate on your everyday life things, as well. You'll be able to focus on the book you're reading, for example; or you'll be able to focus on the job you have to do at work in order to get out a little bit earlier. You'll maximize your life in other ways just by concentrating with greater depth.

3. GREATER ABILITY TO BE CREATIVE.

Recent research from a Netherland-based university notes that people who do open-minded meditation, rather than simply focused-attention meditation, were far more creative and better at coming up with brand new options and ideas.

Therefore, this "creativity" one isn't all-inclusive. You must learn to maximize both focused-attention meditation and open-minded attention in order to fuel maximum creative—and to FOCUS on that creativity. Therefore, there's a sort of yin and yang to the meditation nature and the creative nature. (Note that if you have a great, creative idea for a book, you still need the focus energy in order to complete it.)

4. ENHANCED ABILITY TO REMEMBER.

One of the greatest known results of meditation lies in enhanced memory. Most notably, you have a higher ability to create memory recall as a result of meditation. Note that this was found in a recent research at Martinos Center for Biomedical Imaging. People who practiced daily mindful meditation were able to actively adjust their brain waves, blast away any distractions, and boost their memory output and productivity. Through an enhanced ability to detract all distractions, you are able to remember things, boost your study skills, and build a better mental power. When you remember things, you automatically move up in the world. Just remembering people's names can seriously affect the way you live your life and enhance your self-esteem—and other's thoughts of you.

5. HOLD GREATER COMPASSION FOR PEOPLE.

As discussed in the loving-kindness chapter, much of meditation rallies for greater compassion toward your fellow man. However, it has been shown through scientific research that people who often meditate have higher compassion and empathy levels. This is incredibly important. If you have greater empathy and greater compassion, you are able to handle events and the exterior world on a better, more mature level. When you see bad things in the world, you are able to empathize with the people behind those bad things and thus halt the cycle of bad energy. (Therefore, you won't seek to hurt someone if someone hurts you, etc.)

This is most-notably a result of higher activity in your amygdala, or the essential section of your brain that works through all the stimuli you have as a result of your emotions. Note that this part of the brain is not actually activated during the meditation process; however, there is a sense that this part of the brain is STRENGTHENED during the meditation processes. This is an important distinction to make. Through meditation you are strengthening important neural pathways and giving less power to those that make your life and the lives of others more miserable.

6. A GREATER AMOUNT OF "GRAY MATTER" IN YOUR BRAIN.

Incredibly enough, daily meditation is linked to greater amounts of brain gray matter in both the frontal brain and the hippocampus. When you have more gray matter, or more brain cells, you put yourself in better standing emotionally. You become a more positive, more stable, and more focused person.

Furthermore, meditation has been shown to provide a decreased level of aging on the brain. Therefore, you can hang onto your functionality longer, keep your brain cells vibrant, and avoid serious diseases, like Alzheimer's or dementia. Note that Alzheimer's develops when your brain loses its neural passageways; therefore, your brain cells are unable to "communicate" with each other as readily. When you have more brain matter, this is not such an issue, because it paves the way for more neural passageways.

7. DECREASED LEVELS OF STRESS.

Stress is one of the things that's currently tearing your body apart, limb for limb and brain cell for brain cell. When you turn to meditation—most notably, mindful meditation, rather than open-minded meditation—you can learn to perform better under pressure and feel less stressed while doing it.

According to recent research, after just eight weeks, a group of people who began participating in mindful meditation had less stress than people who did nothing or people who participated in relaxation training. Therefore, mindfulness mediation is the ultimate path toward decreased levels of stress, and it should be turned to for everything from handling your school studies, handling your work stress, handling family stress, and getting through the daily grind in one piece.

Chapter 4. Learning to Meditate: For Beginners

This chapter outlines both the mindfulness of breathing meditation and loving kindness meditation, both of which are essential on the road to recovery and living a better, more organic, and happier life.

How to Meditate Utilizing Buddha's Mindfulness of Breathing

The mindfulness of breathing meditation, or the meditation in which you focus directly on your breathing in order to create interior concentration, works to formulate four stages that ultimately lead to a high level of enjoyment and targeted concentration. Note that the Buddhist Center recommends that you begin with five minutes of concentration in the beginning stages and build your way toward greater periods of concentration time.

The First Stage

During this first stage, you must focus on your breathing utilizing the counting method.

Begin by sitting in a calm, cool, and slightly dark location without anyone around you. Next, begin to breathe in and breathe out, slowly and naturally. After each of your exhales, you say in your mind: "one, two, three," etc. Do this until you reach the number ten. After you reach ten, begin again at one. If you count too high, you begin to get "bogged down" with the passing of time. This way, it's like you're on a constant loop. You lose your sense of time and space, which is essential to dive into the meditative processes.

The Second Stage

During the second stage of mindfulness of breathing, you begin to count directly before your inhale. Therefore, you're concentrating on the anticipation of the next breath rather than the release of the last breath. Continue counting from one to ten, as you did in the first stage, always going back to one after ten. Do this for five minutes when you're a beginner, gradually working up to greater amounts of time as you become practiced in the art of concentration. The importance here is to continue to "target" your focus, rather than allow it to broaden.

The Third Stage

During the third stage, you eliminate the counting element of the concentration. This time, you simply "watch" your breathing from your mind's eye. You inhale and exhale slowly and easily, noticing how your breath comes and goes. Therefore, you're folding yourself away from "listening" to the voice inside your mind. You're allowing a sort of quiet to take hold of you.

The Fourth Stage

During the last stage of the mindfulness of breathing meditation, you have to make your concentration far more intricate, far narrower.

Note that this is quite different from the initial stages. In the first and second stage, for example, you were paying attention to your breathing and your counting. You had a broad scope of concentration. In the third stage, you took away that internal voice and noticed only your breathing. You narrowed your scope of concentration.

In this final stage, you must narrow it even further. As you breath, inhale and exhale, you'll concentrate only on the way the air feels in your nostrils, at your nostrils' very tip, when it enters and exits your body. That is all you are to allow yourself to notice. Remember that learning to control what you notice and what you concentrate on is the sheer message of the mindfulness of breathing meditation style.

How to Meditate Utilizing Loving-Kindness Meditation

When you begin loving-kindness meditation, you must begin to accept yourself, love yourself, and be kind to yourself—otherwise you will not be able to have this experience toward others.

Once you begin to love yourself and orchestrate kindness toward yourself, you can develop loving-kindness toward the following people, most specifically:

1. A person who is a close friend or family member.
2. A person who is deeply respected by you, like a teacher.
3. A person with whom you have no special connection or special hatred. This person could be someone you see every once and a while, like your local barista.
4. A person with whom you often disagree.

When you begin to experience the loving-kindness meditation toward both yourself and the above listed four people, you can begin to burst beyond your mind barriers, break through your mind divisions, and eliminate any interior and external conflict.

1. BEGIN WITH VISUALIZATION.

When you begin the loving-kindness meditation, it is essential that you begin by bringing up a mental portrait.

Therefore, if you are attempting to bring loving-kindness toward yourself, you must picture yourself smiling or feeling joy.

If you are attempting to bring feelings of loving-kindness toward one of the above listed people, on the other hand, you must begin by bringing up a mental image of them either smiling or acting joyously. Note that visualizing things is absolutely the first step to reaching toward that reality.

2. NEXT, ESCALATE TO REFLECTION.

During reflection, you must learn to think about the specific, good qualities of either you or the person to which you're directing these positive feelings. Think about anything kind this person has done for either you or others. If this person is not someone you know very well, you can make something up. Surely you can imagine his or her home life—the life that exists beyond the boundaries you currently have in your relationship with him or her.

Furthermore, state something about yourself that is positive. Use your own description, your owns words about yourself to state something you like, something you've done recently that is positive, etc.

3. UTILIZE AUDITORY MEDITATION.

During this aspect of loving-kindness meditation, you must repeat something in your mind over and over—a mantra or a phrase. Oftentimes, people utilize "loving-kindness."

This auditory state allows you to flow with these loving and kindness feelings, to propel these feelings toward others, and to nurture those feelings within yourself.

Through these devices, you're meant to ultimately "feel" loving and kindness. When you begin to fell these things through these devices, it is essential that you "switch" your focus from your devices to the feeling and focus, instead, on the feelings of love and kindness rather than the journey to get to loving and kindness. If you lose these feelings of love and kindness, you can swiftly switch back to the device you've been using to bring the feelings back. Therefore, you can strengthen your abilities to feel love and kindness while also generating those feelings all the time. Once you generate them enough times, you can swiftly switch to those feelings, no matter where you are or who you're with.

4. *Project Theses Feelings North, South, East, West, Up, and Down.*

After you learn how to feeling loving and kindness, it is essential that you spread those loving kindness feelings to all positions all over the world. Think about friends and family members you might love in various places all over the world to supercharge this ability to send these good vibes all over the world.

Note that this is called Directional Pervasion. However, something called non-specific pervasion generally occurs spontaneously as you begin to strengthen your directional pervasion abilities. Therefore, you'll begin to naturally propel these feelings of kindness and love to all the world, to all people.

Chapter 5. Making meditation a Habit

If you struggle making meditation a habit, just know you're not alone. In fact, people since the dawn of time have struggled with their meditation routine. Because you understand that meditation is absolutely essential for you to live the best version of your life, free from stress, filled with balance, you must fit meditation into your everyday life. But how?

Look to the following meditation tips in order to relive your rushing mind, make meditation an everyday experience, and motivate yourself to always turn to meditation, one of the healthiest things you can do for your body and your mind.

Meditation Tip Number One: Lose Any Concept of Having a Good versus a Bad Meditation

When you're a beginner in the meditation game, it's essential to remember that you can't really "do it wrong." This is good news! Essentially, if you're working through any of the techniques orchestrated in the previous chapter, you can't go wrong. Note that your emotions might always get the best of you; they are like the weather, mashing up your meditation habits. However, if you take the time—through meditation—to NOTICE your mind, the way it's currently rushing, the way you are unable to focus, or the way you're feeling especially sad or depressed lately, you are doing enough. You are making a step toward a long-term commitment to meditation.

Therefore, it's essential that you never, ever evaluate the progress you've made, day-to-day on the meditation sphere. There's no way you can "see" your progress clearly, and if you're having an especially "muddled" day, you might refute everything you've done before and state that you simply haven't created a meditative state—and why should you try in the future? You'll want to avoid this state of mind.

Furthermore, one of the best signs that you HAVE been developing, meditation-wise, is that you notice that your emotions are going wonky. This means that, generally speaking, you have a steady mind when you want to meditate and you have a link, an engagement with your mind. It's only when your mind is a mess of energy that you're "out of it," a little. This can happen. It's best not to get discouraged and to continue formulating a habit.

Meditation Tip Number Two: Learn to Reflect on the Reasons You Meditate

Note that you are committing a good portion of your day to meditation. (For most, it's fifteen to twenty minutes.) But why are you doing this, anyway? Remember that everything you do has a purpose, has a reason. Therefore, it's essential that you focus on the reasons you meditate.

Remember that mediation has been around for thousands of years. Note that modern researchers state that meditation brings enhanced wellbeing and happiness. Furthermore, note that the loving-kindness meditation brings positivity and overall happiness. It can even, on a physiological level, work to calm your heart rate and allow you to live more mindfully, easily, and with greater purpose. It can grow brain cells to reduce aging! Amazing.

Furthermore, note that it's been found that Buddhists are far more rational and realistic when they make money decisions. Therefore, if you're trying to plan your life or work toward a better livelihood, it will behoove you to meditate often. It's simply an appropriate economic choice.

There's a benefit for everyone when it comes to meditation. Everyone has something he or she is passionate about; everyone has something to focus on in the morning, when he or she doesn't want to get out of bed and meditate. There is a purpose and a benefit behind meditation, and you must bring that into your mind and force yourself to follow the path to better your life.

Meditation Tip Number Three: Utilize Some Sort of Exterior Assistant

Buddhists turn to something called malas, or meditation beads, in order to fuel greater concentration when they want to meditate. This further helps them to "count" their mantras. (Funnily enough, many modern-day Buddhists utilize a smart phone app for their "mala." But whatever works, I guess, right?)

Turn to calendars, modern-day habit-training phone applications, Google calendar alerts, a nagging friend, or anything else that makes you understand that you HAVE to meditate because an outside source is going to force you. Note that one of the best ways to "force" yourself to meditate is to buddy up with someone who is also trying to meditate often. When you buddy up, you can pester each other, continually ask if the other person meditated, and monitor each other's progress.

Most research states that if you do meditation habitually for eleven days straight, you will keep it in mind for future dates. Therefore, continue on the meditation trek for at least eleven days and then just SEE if you can quit. Just see.

MEDITATION TIP NUMBER FOUR: FIND A WAY TO MAKE MEDITATION A HABIT RATHER THAN A "MIGHT"

You should never have to force yourself to meditate. It should be just something you do—as easily as washing your hands after you utilize the bathroom or brushing your teeth before you go to bed. It has to be a habit, like anything else, and not something you have to think about, debate, and then, ultimately, decide to do.

Note that habits are created when you do repetitions. Try to meditate every single day at the same exact time to create a sort of interior inertia. Once you wake up, for example, you naturally meditate before anything else.

THE BEGINNER'S BEGINNER'S TWO MINUTES A DAY MEDITATION

So: you really don't want to meditate. You don't want to set aside fifteen minutes every single day. You don't really see the point. You have too many things going on. Whatever.

Listen to this.

You don't have to go all-out, set aside thirty minutes, or even buy one of those "yoga" meditation mats. You don't have to do that. All you have to do is set aside two minutes every single day, at the same time, to "meditate." (Or come up with a different word for it, if you want.) Note that two minutes is the same amount of time it takes the average person to go to the bathroom. It's about the amount of time you have to heat something up in the microwave. It takes no time at all. And then it's over. What do you have to lose, if it means that you might find a pathway to inner peace and excellence?

During these two minutes, you don't need a single thing. All you require is a sort of interior willingness to focus on your mind and your breath. Therefore, you can do this in a chair. You can do this in bed. You can do this in your car. You can do this anywhere.

During these two minutes, simply sit there, wherever you choose to be, and following your breathing. You can do this with either your eyes open or your eyes closed, whichever works the best to initiate yourself to a meditative peace. Allow your breathing to slow, noting how the rest of your body feels as you allow your breathing to lengthen. Become completely and totally conscious of your entire body.

If you have difficulty at first and find yourself in a strange wave of panic about everything you have to do that day, everything you've forgotten about, it is important that you, instead, begin to count your breathing. When you breathe in, count one. When you breathe out, count two. Do this until you reach the level ten, and then go back. This brings a sort of cyclical pattern to your breathing, and it allows your ability to be mindful to attach to your breathing.

Note that you only have to do this for two minutes. Two solid minutes every single day for eleven days. At the end of eleven days, if you've done everything approximately right, you've developed a habit.

But now what?

You can either stick to the two-minute warning rigmarole, OR you can supersede yourself and work toward five-seven minutes. You can eliminate your counting and simply allow yourself to "focus" on your breathing and your body, rather than the numbers. You can gradually escalate to other versions of meditation, as highlighted in the previous chapter.

Just two minutes every single day can absolutely change your life. Do you want to change your life?

Chapter 6. Overarching Benefits and Long-Standing Reasons Why You Should Meditate for Life

Now that you've begun to initiate into meditation, learn the ways in which it can guide you through the rough spots in your life, and keep you deep in reality, you understand: meditation isn't something you can drop from your routine. It's something that you must stick with for life. It's absolutely essential. Remember that every day provides brand new challenges, brand new obstacles, and meditation can keep you on the track to greatness through every hour. It can align your neural pathways to keep you reasonable; it can boost your memory to keep you in the know. It can actually refute aging to keep you upright and "yourself" in the deep days ahead.

Meditation is all you need.

Note the following, overarching benefits and long-standing reasons why you should meditate for life, beyond the pages of this book. Truly, meditation will change your life for the better.

Life-Long Benefits of Meditation

1. Bring Yourself Eternal Ease.

Note that when you're stressed, when the long list of "things you have to do this week" just gets longer and longer, and when you have people nagging at your every move, it can be very, very difficult to stay peaceful, to hold a sense of happiness, a sense of positivity, and a sense of kindness. Even the most meditative, most mentally-charged person can "lose it" sometimes.

However, the best way to cleanse your mind of your stressors and connect yourself back to your sense of purpose is found through daily meditation. You're curing yourself; you're cleansing yourself.

Note that you can utilize meditative techniques beyond your realm of your mat and your "time of the day" for meditation. The next time you feel your heartbeat rising in your chest; the next time you feel like you're getting extra angry, simply turn your focus inward. Begin to focus on your breathing. Begin to focus on a mantra. For example, count your breaths, or say things to your internal mind like: "love and kindness," over and over again.

2. *Fuel a Life with Greater Kindness.*

When you practice meditation, it is true that you're better able to initiate a level of kindness unforeseen. But did you know that you, alongside everyone else you know and love, deserve kindness from yourself as well? Therefore, next time you hear your internal voice put yourself down, you have to halt and begin to focus on your breathing. The next time you feel negatively toward someone you know and leave, begin to focus on your breathing. The next time you feel confused and haughty and upset, simply turn inward, toward your breathing, toward your internal self. Breathe gently and focus on a mantra. Fill yourself with love and kindness toward everyone you know, everyone you don't know, and, of course, yourself.

3. *Allow Yourself to Let Go of Your Internal Dialogue.*

Do you ever want to grab yourself and shut your mind the heck up?

All the time, right? Your mind is always there with consistent doubts, with reasons you shouldn't go for your dreams, with reasons you should meditate, with reasons you should stay in bed—whatever. Your mind can be a consistent demon (even though you should be utilizing it as a tool to initiate into a higher comprehension).

However, if you allow yourself to "let go" a little bit, you can find stillness in your mind. You can find stillness behind the noise of your constant thoughts. Through meditation, you can see your thoughts clearly, as if they're listed before you clearly. You can understand how you actually feel and WHY you feel that why.

When you don't self-reflect about your life, you can't understand yourself as a being in a larger sphere. When you don't self-reflect, you can't understand that nearly everything you do is a reflection of your ego. When you halt your internal ego, you can begin to find concern for the other people in your life, for the people all over the world. You can find true altruism, which, as the Buddha states, is so essential for internal happiness.

4. *Build an Interior Level of Forgiveness.*

So often, we're bogged down with an inability to forgive. We're strapped to past angers, to past fears, and past feelings about ourselves that are no longer relevant. Note, then, that forgiving yourself and others is the number one most essential things you can do.

The next time you meditate, it is important that you watch your thoughts and understand that those thoughts are not the same thoughts you had only moments before. You are not the same person you were five minutes ago, and you were not the same person when you did something so terribly wrong—something you are unable to forgive yourself for.

Therefore, you must bring this comprehension and relate it to everyone else in your life. The person who did something to you is not the same person who exists now, in this moment. People change; people grow. You certainly did, didn't you? Give everyone else this freedom, as well—to grow, to change. And don't expect them to forgive you, necessarily, in return. They might not be at the same level you are, yet.

5. *FALL AWAY FROM FEAR AND ANGER.*

When you have negative feelings, like anger and fear, bottled up in your body, you are very likely to repress them and allow them to bubble up over time—resulting in disaster. Furthermore, this bottling can result in interior depression, shame, and anxiety.

However, when you meditate, you are able to deal with these areas of your mind—these areas of your mind that are bottling your angers and your fears for you. You can see exactly how your mind is actually promoting continued drama in your head. You can see exactly how your mind is promoting your fear of something. For example, if something happened at a particular restaurant three years ago—your boyfriend dumped you, you had a bad salad, whatever—you could have created an aversion to this restaurant in your head. This is a silly example, but it is relevant. When you enter into your mind and understand the ways in which your mind work to alter your feelings and your actions, you can become much more rational moving forward.

You can ultimately swipe away all boundaries in your life and allow yourself to have ultimate awareness about why you make choices and what you really want in life.

6. CREATING A SENSE OF GENTLENESS IN YOUR SOUL

When you create less pain in both your heart and in the hearts of others through enhanced empathy and understanding of the exterior world, you can ultimately bring respect and gentleness in the face of both harm and disrespect. Generally speaking, people enact harm on others without intention. This occurs when people put others down, ignore other people's thoughts and emotions, or insult people without meaning to. This can further occur toward yourself, when you insult yourself or see yourself as unworthy of others' respect.

If you are fueling yourself with large amounts of dislike and shame, then you are ultimately fueling a lack of gentleness in the world and in your heart. When you meditate, you can switch this on its head. You can bring a sense of goodness, of gentleness that will escalate throughout the rest of the world.

7. BRING ETERNAL AWARENESS.

Remember that when you have awareness, you are able to understand the ways in which your mind is attempting to trick you through flying, skirting thoughts and strange thoughts that don't belong. Everything you do is ultimately pegged for an end result, an end consequence. For example, if you work hard at your job, you're doing it to increase your pay grade, feel good about yourself, or get a promotion. If you clean your house, you're doing it to avoid grime, to avoid pathogens, and to feel better on the inside.

However, with meditation, there isn't an "end result" all the time. It's a continuing journey; there's never a destination. You are aware of the world around you; you are aware of your interior mind. You are aware of all space and time, in a sense, and you are able to broaden your mind. You aren't judgmental of yourself or of others. In a sense, for the first time, you are free.

8. Yield a Sense of Appreciation.

When you meditate, you are finally able to appreciate everything you've always taken for granted. As you sit here, reading this, what are you sitting on? A nice, hand-crafted wooden chair? A couch that was created by someone, designed specifically to sit in your living room? Think about every person that was involved in the clothing you currently have hanging on your body. Think about your haircut. Who cut it? Think about every class that person had to go through to learn how to cut hair.

Appreciate every process that the world has to go through on a daily basis to keep you happy, to keep you healthy, and to keep you strong. Appreciate your food; appreciate your energy.

When you appreciate every little thing, you won't want for anything. You'll feel the world open up to you, and you'll accept and appreciate everything it has to offer.

You'll have all you need.

About The Author

My mission with this is to be able to help inspire and change the world, one reader at a time.

I want to provide the most amazing life tools that anyone can apply into their lives. It doesn't matter whether you have hit rock bottom in your life or your life is amazing and you want to keep taking it to another level.

If you are like me, then you are probably looking to become the best version of yourself. You are likely not to settle for an okay life. You want to live an extraordinary life. Not only to be filled within but also to contribute to society.

FREE PREVIEW OF

MOTIVATION:

GETTING MOTIVATED, FEELING MOTIVATED, STAYING MOTIVATED

JUSTIN ALBERT

Copyright © 2014 by Justin Albert

Why You Should Read This Book

Motivation provides ultimate life fulfillment. It is the driving force behind every profession, every physical action. It fuels the creation of towering skyscrapers, five-star restaurant, and stellar paintings—

And yet: why is motivation so difficult to attain and maintain? Another thing: why is it so difficult to get out of bed? When did life get so out of hand?

This book analyzes these questions on both a scientific and emotional level. It lends the proper tools to build motivation in the wake of utter difficulty.

Motivation is pumping in every blood vessel, through every neuron. Human ancestors struggling to survive in the wild were fueled with this instinct: this motivation to persevere. Present people still pulse with this very intrinsic motivation. However, present-day people—because their needs are generally met, their food is generally supplied—must work for their motivation. They must keep eyes open; they must create their own understanding of their goals. Their goal is no longer: survive. Their goal is to prosper.

Procrastination. Stress. The dog needs walking, the cat needs fed. The work piles up, and motivation for desires and interests is simply out of reach. This Motivation E-book teaches the art of catching desires and interests once again and persevering. It outlines the ways one can work through the blocks in your path and attain that promotion, achieve that great legacy. One must do this: reach for real, vibrant goals in order to attain real destiny—to know self-actualization. Only with self-actualization can one feel a renewed sense of prosperity, a full sense of self.

Chapter 1. Motivation: The Only Road to Greatness

Humankind's all-inclusive goal is, effectively, one thing: to survive. The survival concept lurks behind all things in a person's life: behind every kitchen product, behind every home improvement store. And yet, naturally, this survival has changed over the years. It has diminished from something broad, something that must meet required caloric values and required habitat-levels into something much more refined.

What is, then, man's essential, present-day goal? To simply live. And to live well. To live better than man has before. And this goal requires innovation; it requires a push against the limits surrounding each person's life. Without breadth of motivation, people would not leave their beds; they wouldn't work to find a better life. Without motivation, people would have nothing.

Motivation is the call to action. It is the thing that pushes one from one's bed to greet the world and squeeze every ounce of energy from it. It is the thing that forces one to take one's proper stance in the world.

Do you feel, today, that you have the depth of motivation to reach your goals, to push yourself to the top of your career and become a prime person—a person with both physical and mental strength? Do you have the will to survive and the motivation to make the most of that survival?

Understand motivation and the current factors blocking you from your complete embrace of your goals. Understand the ways in which you can become the best version of yourself.

WHAT IS MOTIVATION?

Understanding the precise utilization of motivation is essential in order to prescribe everyday life goals; prescribing life goals via motivation allows for forward-motion.

DEFINITION OF MOTIVATION

Motivation, essentially, is that which initiates and maintains goal-driven mannerisms. It is an unseen force. Biological, cognitive, and social effects alter motivation; these forces mold it, form it into something that either allows growth or stagnation.

Biological effects on motivation involve the various mechanisms required at a very physical level. As aforementioned, one has kitchen appliances that rev and whir in order to maintain a very base biological motive: to boost one's caloric intake for further survival. One reaches for a glass of Coca Cola, essentially, out of motivation to quench one's thirst. These motives are incredibly basic and biological; the animals and plants of the earth have similar biological motivations, as well. A human simply has refined his reach to maintain these motivations.

Cognitive effects on motivation are incredibly complicated. Hormonal imbalances, the things one eats and the things by which one is surrounded can affect the brain, thus altering one's motivational output. Depression, stress, and low self-esteems accumulate at this cognitive level and impair judgment, thus altering continued rev for motivation.

Social effects on motivation generally involve one's environment and cultural influence. What is expected of one in one's culture generally contributes to one's sense of motivation; for example, history finds women generally staying home with children. Their motivation could not grow due to social influences. Furthermore, one's parents and one's friends alter social motivation. If one lives in a stagnant environment—an environment featuring people without conscious effort, without conscious forward-motion, one might simply assimilate into this way of life. However, if one's parents expect certain successes, social motivation might be the factor contributing to one's college graduation, for example.

THREE COMPONENTS OF MOTIVATION

1) Activation
2) Persistence
3) Intensity

Activation is the primary component: the decision to begin. A person must make this conscious decision; it is the root of all motivation. It is the very thing that allows mature motivation to grow. For example, actively enrolling in an exercise class activates the motivation to become healthy and lose weight, thus improving one's life.

Persistence is the continuation of this activation. It involves one's push through obstacles after the initial activation. It involves intense, psychological strength. For example, after one enrolls in the exercise class with the obvious intention of becoming healthy and thin, persistence must step in to truly fuel motivation. After the exercise class begins, one must invest endless hours, limitless concentration, and physicality to the point of exhaustion. It is increasingly difficult to maintain the intensity. However, if one is fueled with the proper motivation, working through the exercise class until completion garners significant strength and benefits.

Finally, intensity measures one's level of vigor after initially activating and persisting. If one persists through the various exercise classes, for example, without a significant level of concentration and exertion, one is not truly motivated. One can persist, certainly. But one will not reach the final goal of true health and strength without full-throttle intensity. Find another example in university-level classes. One can activate one's enrollment; one can attend every class; but if one does not fuel every day with study and push one's self outside of class, one will probably not achieve maximum success.

Extrinsic Motivation versus Intrinsic Motivation

Motivation is found both extrinsically and intrinsically.

Extrinsic motivation exists outside the individual. Usually, it involves the motivation to pursue exterior rewards or trophies—things resulting from successes involving other people. Therefore, extrinsic motivation involves motivation from peers; it involves impressing others via one's success. One's competitive desire can drive this extrinsic motivation completely.

Intrinsic motivation, on the other hand, exists internally. The internal gratification of completing a very personal project, for example, fuels this intrinsic motivation. Perhaps one wants to finish cleaning and decorating one's bedroom simply to feel the fresh, open understanding that one's habitat is for one's self; one's habitat reflects one's life, after all. However, if one simply wants to decorate one's room in order to impress another person, this could deem extrinsic motivation. Essentially, if one is the sole operator of one's motivation without exterior benefit, one is fueled with intrinsic motivation.

A Life Without Motivation: What Happens?

What happens without that pulsing drive of motivation? Where does this lack of motivation lead? Remember that motivation is the building block for all survival, all strength in existence. Furthermore, it is the real push behind desire and interest. It is the very thing that fuels the beautiful paintings in museums, the towering skyscrapers, and the countless football games. It is human's driving force toward the meaning of life.

Feelings of Failure and Inadequacy

Without motivation, one cannot move forward with one's life. One must remain stagnant. Essentially, one's hometown becomes one's only town. One's first job becomes one's only job. Lack of motivation leads nowhere.

But this lack of push does not lead to a lack of feeling. Emotion is always at play. In fact, emotion is generally the pulse behind lack of motivation. These emotions come in forms like fear of failure, fear of the unknown, incredible stresses, and low self-esteem. If one cannot work through these emotions, one cannot build a solid motivational ground. And without this ground and garnered goals, failure and inadequacy sweep into the emotional mix. One can feel a loss: like the past few years of one's life went toward nothing. One can feel a desire to do it all over again—with that drive of motivation at their backs. Unfortunately, lost years don't come back around. And inadequacy and feelings of failure linger.

Fortunately, these feelings of inadequacy can be the very reason to push toward motivation and reach toward something else. Proper use of feelings is always important. Work toward the promotion you haven't even dreamed about; wonder why you never thought to go to the gym. Understand that there's a whole world out there waiting for you. Claim it.

Chapter 2. Theories of Motivation

Psychologists' motivation analysis involves several theories. They analyze the precise reasons why one is fueled with motivation—and why one may have difficulty jumping on the motivation train.

Drive Theory

Behaviorist Clark Hull created the drive reduction theory of motivation in the 1940s and 1950s. He was one of the first scientists to attempt to understand the broad depth of human motivation.

Homeostasis: Balance and Equilibrium

Hull's theories attend to the facts of homeostasis. Homeostasis is the fact that one's body constantly works to achieve balance, equilibrium. For example, one's body finds a consistent, approximate temperature of 98.6 degrees Fahrenheit. When one dips below or above this number, one's body hustles to achieve balance once more.

Essentially, the "drive" of drive theory refers to the tension aroused by the imbalance or lack of homeostasis in one's body. In the temperature case, therefore, one's interior drive is the fact that one's temperature is out of whack. Further drives are hunger and thirst. These drives, or stimuli, force one's body into action to achieve balance in the form of a meal or a glass of water.

Therefore, Hull's drive theory acts on a sort of stimulus-response mechanism. His theory is rooted in biology and therefore takes no notice of interior, life goals. However, he does provide a decent understanding of the root of motivation.

INSTINCT THEORY

Psychologist William McDougall studied the instinct theory in relation to human motivation. His essential findings rooted the instinct theory as a way through life—a way that assured continuation of life via natural selection. Of course, the behaviors he studied were not limited to biological needs. He studied human instinct; and human instinct garners several shades of gray.

WHAT IS AN INSTINCT?

An instinct involves a tendency to behave in a specific manner without engaging in thought. The acts are spontaneous, occurring in a sort of matter of course after a particular occurrence.

Human instincts cover a broad range of occurrences rooted in both physiological and psychological needs. Physiological motivations, of course, meet hunger, thirst, and habitation needs. Psychological motivations, however, clasp something a bit more human; things like: humor, curiosity, cleanliness, fear, anger, shame, and love.

MASLOW'S HIERARCHY OF NEEDS

Abraham Maslow's humanistic theory of motivation analyzes all the basic human elements—from the simplistic biological needs to the self-actualization needs.

He breaks these needs into five stages with the idea that one's motivations can only escalate when one's needs are met at the immediate stages.

Stage 1: Physiological Needs

As aforementioned, physiological needs consist of the basic, survival needs like water, food, and sleep. One must meet these physiological needs prior to building the motivation to move to the next step.

Stage 2: Safety Needs

These safety needs involve providing one's self with proper health, income, and an actual "home."

Stage 3: Love/Belonging Needs

After one meets physiological needs and one has a place to live, a place in which to feel whole, one can begin to understand the benefits of social surroundings. These benefits can fall from familial ties, friendship, work groups— anything that forms a sort of relationship in which one can beat back against loneliness and find a place in society.

Stage 4: Self-Esteem Needs

One jumps to the self esteem needs stage in the convenient stage after one feels a sense of belonging. Learning that one "fits" in a society is a great link in the chain. Self-esteem needs allow one the motivation to achieve in one's school or work and to build one's reputation. It allows one to take responsibility of other things or other people. This is essential in the hierarchy of needs: that one does not "need" anything anymore—one is motivated, instead, to help other people meet their needs. One is further motivated to meet one's wants.

Stage 5: Self-Actualization Needs

Self-actualization involves something a bit deeper than the self-esteem stage. The self-esteem stage requires one to achieve in society, to take charge of one's self and one's life. However, the self-actualization stage motivates one to find personal growth, it motivates one to feel fulfilled by one's career, one's relationships. It might not be enough, for example, for one to simply achieve at one's job. This stage might require one to feel as if one's commitment to one's job is also making the world a better place, for example. One might do some soul-searching in this stage to truly understand one's place in the world. One cannot commit to this true soul-searching, of course, without meeting the initial four stages of the hierarchy of needs. However, to truly find one's self and truly meet one's goals, one must exist at this top stage—with all other needs completed.

Keep reading...

MOTIVATION:

GETTING MOTIVATED, FEELING MOTIVATED, STAYING MOTIVATED

OTHER BOOKS BY: JUSTIN ALBERT

SPORTS PSYCHOLOGY: INSIDE THE ATHLETE'S MIND

Have You Ever Wanted To Improve Your Performance? No matter what sport you play, there are always problems with confidence and motivation that can get in the way of actually using all of the skills that you have been working to build through your entire life. That is where sports psychology comes in.

With the help of this book, you will be able to:
Build confidence that helps you become unstoppable.
Visualize your way to success so that you know what to expect.

Set goals that will help you measure improvements and strive towards specific markers.

Learn how to help others to do the same.
By combining simple techniques with a high quality understanding of psychology, you will have everything at your disposal to take your performance to the next level and find success that you never thought possible previously.

SOCIAL PSYCHOLOGY: A PRACTICAL GUIDE TO THE HUMAN MIND

Understanding why people do what they do is an essential skills to have. When you understand why the people around you do what they do, you are able to avoid a lot of drama and conflict.

Throughout history society has had a profound influence in people's actions

This book was written to fulfill a simple mission: to educate people from all walks of life about the importance and application of social psychology in their day-to-day lives.

This book was not written to make science intimidating, not to mention boring. The aim is to show how a serious and legitimate science like social psychology could be easily understood and appreciated by non-psychology majors, practically by every 'man on the street'.

Are you any of the following?
Simply curious about how human minds work, especially in a group or social setting, but won't bother digging complicated science stuff
Wants to have something productive to do during free time, regardless of what it is
A freshman/woman in a general psychology major
Undecided on what major to take in university/college

If any, this book is for you!

Cognitive Behavioral Therapy: CBT Essentials and Fundamentals

There's no reason to live a life without fulfillment or excitement. In our modern world, we see people struggling with depression, anxiety, anger, etc. Psychologist and counselors have been using Cognitive Behavioral Therapy to solve all these struggles.
A Practical Guide to CBT and Modern Psychology will allow anyone to use CBT in their lives.

It doesn't matter whether or not you have a background in Psychology. In this comprehensive guide you will learn all the fundamentals used in CBT by therapists.

Inside you will be exposed to the following:

CBT History
Techniques
When and How to use CBT
Example's
Methods to help others with psychological struggles

And much more

If you're ready to understand and use the powerful techniques of Cognitive Behavioral Therapy, then this is an excellent guide.

Emotional Intelligence: A Practical Guide to Mastering Emotions: Emotions Handbook and Journal

Understanding emotions is one of the most important aspects of personal development and growth

Without truly mastering our emotions we run a high risk in behaving without awareness.

Throughout years society has come to believe that our level of IQ will determine the success of a person's life. However, in recent years psychologist have found new insight by studying successful people. The results have been surprising because what determines a person's life success is not IQ but rather EI.

Emotional Intelligence (EI) is the foundation of living a successful and meaningful life. People who succeed in life have a tremendous awareness of their emotions.

Inside this book, you will be on the path of living a life that includes the following

Emotional Mastery

Awareness of your own emotions and others

Effortlessly redirecting your emotions

A deeper connection with the people you love

Do not allow your emotions to take over your life and instead master the art of your emotions today!

Motivation: Getting Motivated, Feeling Motivated, Staying Motivated

Confidence: Build Unbreakable, Unstoppable, Powerful Confidence: Boost Your Confidence: A 21-Day Challenge

Spirituality: A Search for Balance and Enlightenment: Spiritual Health and Wellness

FREE PREVIEW OF

MOTIVATION:

GETTING MOTIVATED, FEELING MOTIVATED, STAYING MOTIVATED

JUSTIN ALBERT

Copyright © 2014 by Justin Albert

Why You Should Read This Book

Motivation provides ultimate life fulfillment. It is the driving force behind every profession, every physical action. It fuels the creation of towering skyscrapers, five-star restaurant, and stellar paintings—

And yet: why is motivation so difficult to attain and maintain? Another thing: why is it so difficult to get out of bed? When did life get so out of hand?

This book analyzes these questions on both a scientific and emotional level. It lends the proper tools to build motivation in the wake of utter difficulty.

Motivation is pumping in every blood vessel, through every neuron. Human ancestors struggling to survive in the wild were fueled with this instinct: this motivation to persevere. Present people still pulse with this very intrinsic motivation. However, present-day people—because their needs are generally met, their food is generally supplied—must work for their motivation. They must keep eyes open; they must create their own understanding of their goals. Their goal is no longer: survive. Their goal is to prosper.

Procrastination. Stress. The dog needs walking, the cat needs fed. The work piles up, and motivation for desires and interests is simply out of reach. This Motivation E-book teaches the art of catching desires and interests once again and persevering. It outlines the ways one can work through the blocks in your path and attain that promotion, achieve that great legacy. One must do this: reach for real, vibrant goals in order to attain real destiny—to know self-actualization. Only with self-actualization can one feel a renewed sense of prosperity, a full sense of self.

Chapter 1. Motivation: The Only Road to Greatness

Humankind's all-inclusive goal is, effectively, one thing: to survive. The survival concept lurks behind all things in a person's life: behind every kitchen product, behind every home improvement store. And yet, naturally, this survival has changed over the years. It has diminished from something broad, something that must meet required caloric values and required habitat-levels into something much more refined.

What is, then, man's essential, present-day goal? To simply live. And to live well. To live better than man has before. And this goal requires innovation; it requires a push against the limits surrounding each person's life. Without breadth of motivation, people would not leave their beds; they wouldn't work to find a better life. Without motivation, people would have nothing.

Motivation is the call to action. It is the thing that pushes one from one's bed to greet the world and squeeze every ounce of energy from it. It is the thing that forces one to take one's proper stance in the world.

Do you feel, today, that you have the depth of motivation to reach your goals, to push yourself to the top of your career and become a prime person—a person with both physical and mental strength? Do you have the will to survive and the motivation to make the most of that survival?

Understand motivation and the current factors blocking you from your complete embrace of your goals. Understand the ways in which you can become the best version of yourself.

WHAT IS MOTIVATION?

Understanding the precise utilization of motivation is essential in order to prescribe everyday life goals; prescribing life goals via motivation allows for forward-motion.

DEFINITION OF MOTIVATION

Motivation, essentially, is that which initiates and maintains goal-driven mannerisms. It is an unseen force. Biological, cognitive, and social effects alter motivation; these forces mold it, form it into something that either allows growth or stagnation.

Biological effects on motivation involve the various mechanisms required at a very physical level. As aforementioned, one has kitchen appliances that rev and whir in order to maintain a very base biological motive: to boost one's caloric intake for further survival. One reaches for a glass of Coca Cola, essentially, out of motivation to quench one's thirst. These motives are incredibly basic and biological; the animals and plants of the earth have similar biological motivations, as well. A human simply has refined his reach to maintain these motivations.

Cognitive effects on motivation are incredibly complicated. Hormonal imbalances, the things one eats and the things by which one is surrounded can affect the brain, thus altering one's motivational output. Depression, stress, and low self-esteems accumulate at this cognitive level and impair judgment, thus altering continued rev for motivation.

Social effects on motivation generally involve one's environment and cultural influence. What is expected of one in one's culture generally contributes to one's sense of motivation; for example, history finds women generally staying home with children. Their motivation could not grow due to social influences. Furthermore, one's parents and one's friends alter social motivation. If one lives in a stagnant environment—an environment featuring people without conscious effort, without conscious forward-motion, one might simply assimilate into this way of life. However, if one's parents expect certain successes, social motivation might be the factor contributing to one's college graduation, for example.

THREE COMPONENTS OF MOTIVATION

1) Activation
2) Persistence
3) Intensity

Activation is the primary component: the decision to begin. A person must make this conscious decision; it is the root of all motivation. It is the very thing that allows mature motivation to grow. For example, actively enrolling in an exercise class activates the motivation to become healthy and lose weight, thus improving one's life.

Persistence is the continuation of this activation. It involves one's push through obstacles after the initial activation. It involves intense, psychological strength. For example, after one enrolls in the exercise class with the obvious intention of becoming healthy and thin, persistence must step in to truly fuel motivation. After the exercise class begins, one must invest endless hours, limitless concentration, and physicality to the point of exhaustion. It is increasingly difficult to maintain the intensity. However, if one is fueled with the proper motivation, working through the exercise class until completion garners significant strength and benefits.

Finally, intensity measures one's level of vigor after initially activating and persisting. If one persists through the various exercise classes, for example, without a significant level of concentration and exertion, one is not truly motivated. One can persist, certainly. But one will not reach the final goal of true health and strength without full-throttle intensity. Find another example in university-level classes. One can activate one's enrollment; one can attend every class; but if one does not fuel every day with study and push one's self outside of class, one will probably not achieve maximum success.

Extrinsic Motivation versus Intrinsic Motivation

Motivation is found both extrinsically and intrinsically.

Extrinsic motivation exists outside the individual. Usually, it involves the motivation to pursue exterior rewards or trophies—things resulting from successes involving other people. Therefore, extrinsic motivation involves motivation from peers; it involves impressing others via one's success. One's competitive desire can drive this extrinsic motivation completely.

Intrinsic motivation, on the other hand, exists internally. The internal gratification of completing a very personal project, for example, fuels this intrinsic motivation. Perhaps one wants to finish cleaning and decorating one's bedroom simply to feel the fresh, open understanding that one's habitat is for one's self; one's habitat reflects one's life, after all. However, if one simply wants to decorate one's room in order to impress another person, this could deem extrinsic motivation. Essentially, if one is the sole operator of one's motivation without exterior benefit, one is fueled with intrinsic motivation.

A Life Without Motivation: What Happens?

What happens without that pulsing drive of motivation? Where does this lack of motivation lead? Remember that motivation is the building block for all survival, all strength in existence. Furthermore, it is the real push behind desire and interest. It is the very thing that fuels the beautiful paintings in museums, the towering skyscrapers, and the countless football games. It is human's driving force toward the meaning of life.

Feelings of Failure and Inadequacy

Without motivation, one cannot move forward with one's life. One must remain stagnant. Essentially, one's hometown becomes one's only town. One's first job becomes one's only job. Lack of motivation leads nowhere.

But this lack of push does not lead to a lack of feeling. Emotion is always at play. In fact, emotion is generally the pulse behind lack of motivation. These emotions come in forms like fear of failure, fear of the unknown, incredible stresses, and low self-esteem. If one cannot work through these emotions, one cannot build a solid motivational ground. And without this ground and garnered goals, failure and inadequacy sweep into the emotional mix. One can feel a loss: like the past few years of one's life went toward nothing. One can feel a desire to do it all over again—with that drive of motivation at their backs. Unfortunately, lost years don't come back around. And inadequacy and feelings of failure linger.

Fortunately, these feelings of inadequacy can be the very reason to push toward motivation and reach toward something else. Proper use of feelings is always important. Work toward the promotion you haven't even dreamed about; wonder why you never thought to go to the gym. Understand that there's a whole world out there waiting for you. Claim it.

Chapter 2. Theories of Motivation

Psychologists' motivation analysis involves several theories. They analyze the precise reasons why one is fueled with motivation—and why one may have difficulty jumping on the motivation train.

Drive Theory

Behaviorist Clark Hull created the drive reduction theory of motivation in the 1940s and 1950s. He was one of the first scientists to attempt to understand the broad depth of human motivation.

Homeostasis: Balance and Equilibrium

Hull's theories attend to the facts of homeostasis. Homeostasis is the fact that one's body constantly works to achieve balance, equilibrium. For example, one's body finds a consistent, approximate temperature of 98.6 degrees Fahrenheit. When one dips below or above this number, one's body hustles to achieve balance once more.

Essentially, the "drive" of drive theory refers to the tension aroused by the imbalance or lack of homeostasis in one's body. In the temperature case, therefore, one's interior drive is the fact that one's temperature is out of whack. Further drives are hunger and thirst. These drives, or stimuli, force one's body into action to achieve balance in the form of a meal or a glass of water.

Therefore, Hull's drive theory acts on a sort of stimulus-response mechanism. His theory is rooted in biology and therefore takes no notice of interior, life goals. However, he does provide a decent understanding of the root of motivation.

INSTINCT THEORY

Psychologist William McDougall studied the instinct theory in relation to human motivation. His essential findings rooted the instinct theory as a way through life—a way that assured continuation of life via natural selection. Of course, the behaviors he studied were not limited to biological needs. He studied human instinct; and human instinct garners several shades of gray.

What Is An Instinct?

An instinct involves a tendency to behave in a specific manner without engaging in thought. The acts are spontaneous, occurring in a sort of matter of course after a particular occurrence.

Human instincts cover a broad range of occurrences rooted in both physiological and psychological needs. Physiological motivations, of course, meet hunger, thirst, and habitation needs. Psychological motivations, however, clasp something a bit more human; things like: humor, curiosity, cleanliness, fear, anger, shame, and love.

MASLOW'S HIERARCHY OF NEEDS

Abraham Maslow's humanistic theory of motivation analyzes all the basic human elements—from the simplistic biological needs to the self-actualization needs.

He breaks these needs into five stages with the idea that one's motivations can only escalate when one's needs are met at the immediate stages.

STAGE 1: PHYSIOLOGICAL NEEDS

As aforementioned, physiological needs consist of the basic, survival needs like water, food, and sleep. One must meet these physiological needs prior to building the motivation to move to the next step.

STAGE 2: SAFETY NEEDS

These safety needs involve providing one's self with proper health, income, and an actual "home."

STAGE 3: LOVE/BELONGING NEEDS

After one meets physiological needs and one has a place to live, a place in which to feel whole, one can begin to understand the benefits of social surroundings. These benefits can fall from familial ties, friendship, work groups—anything that forms a sort of relationship in which one can beat back against loneliness and find a place in society.

Stage 4: Self-Esteem Needs

One jumps to the self esteem needs stage in the convenient stage after one feels a sense of belonging. Learning that one "fits" in a society is a great link in the chain. Self-esteem needs allow one the motivation to achieve in one's school or work and to build one's reputation. It allows one to take responsibility of other things or other people. This is essential in the hierarchy of needs: that one does not "need" anything anymore—one is motivated, instead, to help other people meet their needs. One is further motivated to meet one's wants.

Stage 5: Self-Actualization Needs

Self-actualization involves something a bit deeper than the self-esteem stage. The self-esteem stage requires one to achieve in society, to take charge of one's self and one's life. However, the self-actualization stage motivates one to find personal growth, it motivates one to feel fulfilled by one's career, one's relationships. It might not be enough, for example, for one to simply achieve at one's job. This stage might require one to feel as if one's commitment to one's job is also making the world a better place, for example. One might do some soul-searching in this stage to truly understand one's place in the world. One cannot commit to this true soul-searching, of course, without meeting the initial four stages of the hierarchy of needs. However, to truly find one's self and truly meet one's goals, one must exist at this top stage—with all other needs completed.

ONE LAST THING...

If you enjoyed this book or found it useful I'd be very grateful if you'd post a short review on Amazon. Your support really does make a difference and I read all the reviews personally so I can get your feedback and make this book even better.

Thanks again for your support!

Printed in Great Britain
by Amazon